A Murder of

Crows

& Other Poems

Other Books by the Author

Healthy Baking: Gluten-free,
Wheat-free, Dairy-free

Specialty Muffins and Pancakes: Gluten-
free, Wheat-free, Dairy-free

Specialty Cookies: Gluten-free,
Wheat-free, Dairy-free

Holiday Treats

Dark Chocolate Delights

A Murder of
Crows
& Other Poems

Deborah Hanula

Tellwell Talent
www.tellwell.ca

ISBN
978-0-2288-8820-8 (Hardcover)
978-0-2288-8821-5 (Paperback)
978-0-2288-8819-2 (eBook)

Dedications

To Nathaniel who believed and inspired.
To Michael who sorted through some
technical glitches with me.

Table of Contents

Poetry

Haikus

Part One

Poetry

Darkness Fell and I Was Scared

Darkness fell and I was scared
Terrified
Worried about what would happen when he
arrived home.

I would have to hide in the attic trunk
A curly-haired little girl
Wearing a peach-coloured nightie
With my little blonde doll
Clutched to my chest
In the darkness of the musty wood
Shaking
Quiet
Afraid to breathe.

He would scream in a rage that he did not
want us
Did not want to be married
Had never wanted a child
And he would threaten to leave us once and
for all.

She would scream back at him
To please leave us
Leave us alone
And never come back
That we could survive without him
And his drunken stench
Blended with the cheap perfume of his sexual
    liaisons
And the acrid smell of his vomit
That she cleaned up only after he passed out
At least a few times a week
His curses, humiliations, spittle and raging fists
Aimed at her chest, cheeks, ears, lips and eyes
And the repeated sexual violations
The trauma.

And he would ask where I was
And she would lie
Say that I was at a sleepover
Across town.

He never looked for me
I don't think he had it in him to climb up three
    flights of stairs to the attic
I was safe
At least I silently prayed that I would be
But I worried that he was going to kill her this
    time
That I wouldn't have a mommy to protect me
Then he would do to me what he was doing
    to her

And I fervently prayed to please spare her
To protect her
Protect me
Stop him in his tracks with a bolt of lightning.

One day he left
He really did leave us
For many months
We heard nothing
Saw nothing
Thought that we were safe
We could carry on
Rebuild
We hoped that he had left the city
Moved on
Tired and bored of tormenting us
Perhaps had gone back to the farm he'd grown
      up on
Smack dab in the middle of the dusty, seemingly
      endless prairies.

But on a warm and gentle spring evening
We heard a strange scratching at the handle
Of our new, steel-reinforced front door
Like someone who was trying to get a key to fit
      into a lock
That it no longer fit into.

We heard a pause
Then we heard his voice
Slowly, deliberately, reading out loud

The words of the restraining order
Posted on the door
Warning him to stay away
From our house
From us.

She had added her own note
Stating that she had a gun
And would shoot him
If he broke into our house
Tried to get to us.

I heard him guffaw with disbelief
Followed by a roar of sardonic laughter
Which slowly, painfully turned into the guttural
    rasping
Of what sounded like a dying animal.

We had already called the police
They were on their way
They arrived and took him with them
Because he was not keeping the peace
And had breached the court order.

After I grew up and created a family of my own
Had moved to a different part of the country
The telephone mounted on the kitchen wall
    trilled one day
And I learned on that soft, warm, summer
    afternoon

While sipping a tall glass of cool, lemon water
    with the receiver to my ear
Looking through the window over my kitchen
    sink
Delighting in all the splendour of nature right
    outside my house
The hum of the honey bees
Amidst the colourful blooms in the gardens
And the darting of the dragonflies
Accompanied by the whistling of the robins and
    the chirping of the chickadees
The gentle love songs of life.

That he had finally gotten to her
Exactly one week from the day he was released
    from prison
After knifing a guy in a bar fight and serving
    time
In a small northern town.

Her new mate
A kind, loving, gentle partner of just over a year
Had opened the door to what he thought was a
    salesman of some sort or another
She was right behind him
With a friendly smile
To see who was at the door
No one had alerted her to his release
She was not the reason he ended up doing time
    after all
So it crossed no one's mind to warn her.

She was barefoot
Her long, silver-streaked hair tied back with a
    blue, silk ribbon
Looking radiant in a shin-length, bright yellow
    summer smock
Printed with white, yellow-centered daisies
Carefree
Loved
At peace
Until the shock of seeing him.

He shot them both at close range
Dropped the gun
And strolled away.

Cold Enough

I can't wait until it's cold enough
to bring my frozen stiff long johns in from the
clothesline.

I'll soak in my hot tub surrounded by drifts of
snow and marvel at white-capped mountains in
the hazy distance.

I'll make a snow angel after dark as I gaze
upwards at millions of twinkling stars in our
galaxy.

I'll stick my tongue onto an aluminum railing
only to scream out in agony
(and some delight)
while ripping it free from its icy hold.

No Voice

She wanted to say to him
that his choices were designed to inflict
maximum psychological harm on her
but her throat seized up
and all she could utter
were the gasps of a tiny, withered baby sparrow.

Gifts of My Father

During my childhood, the greatest gift my father
    gave me was his lack of criticism.
During my university years, the greatest gift my
    father gave me was his strength.
During my adult years, the greatest gift my father
    gave me was his delight in my son.

And the thread that connected all these things
    and many more throughout the years
was the love that emanated from his eyes when
    he looked at me.

Laura

Laura lay in bed
massaging her belly
as wave after wave of sharp abdominal pain
followed by nausea
relentlessly washed over her
she was feverish
and drenched in sweat
how long it had gone on for
she wasn't exactly sure
seven hours perhaps
she thought
as she glanced at the clock-radio
on her bedside table
though it felt like days.

Her doctor had advised her
to keep using birth control even now
as she finished progressing through menopause
but she didn't feel the need to
because her self-absorbed, career-focused
    husband
hadn't deigned to even touch her

for at least five years now
and during rare occasions when she caught him
    looking at her
his face held a mixture of disgust and
    indifference
even though she had aged well
keeping herself slim and trim
toned and youthful
through vigorous exercise and healthy eating
it wasn't her that he wanted anymore
as his weeks were occupied in distant cities
with a smorgasbord of all the young flesh he
    could take pleasure in.

One night though
a couple of months ago
her husband stumbled into her room after a few
    too many whiskey sours
and before she was quite awake enough to figure
    out what was happening
with a thrust
he was inside of her.

She just lay there
waiting for it to be over
barely breathing
feeling odd
detached
and ever so slightly as if she was being raped
had she consented
was consent implicit because he was her husband

she was groggy and couldn't really get her mind
    to work logically
she tried to force her brain to solve the legality of
    what was happening to her
but the more she tried to force an answer the less
    she could think.

He was in his early sixties and his penis was not
    very hard
somewhat limp in fact
no doubt partly due to the alcohol he reeked of
it took great effort on his part for him to ejaculate
but he did
eventually
and left what was once their bed.

Their love had died years ago
he was rarely ever home and when he was
    around
there was only great distance between them
in her case
she had completely shut down
numbed herself
in order to simply survive from day to day.

Now this.

Her baby
their baby
suctioned out from inside of her
she had been pro-choice from as far back as she
    could remember

since the issue first reared its head on campus
her choice
she always thought
would never be 'yes' for herself
but the doctor said that she was far too old to
     deliver a healthy baby
she was putting herself at risk
and the baby would most likely have extreme
     health issues
possibly be misshapen, ill-formed, chronically ill
in need of round-the-clock care
if it even lived
a half-human lump of some sort she imagined
as the doctor's voice faded away and the ringing
     in her ears intensified.

She hadn't told her husband that she was
     pregnant
it wasn't as if he would be happy and supportive
she envisioned an intensified look of disgust in
     her direction.

His betrayals began years ago
and over time
he became no more to her than a speck of dust
     that she could never quite get rid of
the one that drifts in and out of view
based on where the light happens to be striking
     the floor
as sunlight pours in through an open window.

The few times she had to be together with him in
    public were excruciating
as she watched him puff himself up
then ogle every young woman with legs, an ass
and long blonde hair
their faces could be repulsive
but as long as the legs and ass were there
and the long blonde hair
and they were young and ripe
that's all that seemed to matter to him.

Her doctor told her
that it was the anger she felt towards her husband
that she refused to express
that was making her feel nauseated
even before the pregnancy did
her husband's true colours were ugly and she,
    too, was now ugly
her soul was dark
her thoughts were abhorrent
she had become a wretched person both inside
    and out
and spent most of her time hiding alone in her
    house
an old hag of a middle-aged woman.

But at this moment
after hours of pain and nausea
all that Laura could do
was gently rock back and forth
holding her knees to her chest
and whimper

ever so softly
ever so gently
ever so quietly
to ensure that even God couldn't hear her.

My Sweet Child

Though my eyes are dim
I know your face
I've scanned it with my fingertips
countless times.

Your flattened nose
almond-shaped eyes
and chubby cheeks
have mesmerized me.

You are usually very patient
and don't seem to mind
keeping silent and still until my fingertips tickle
or you simply become too bored.

This ritual cements our bond.

They tell me that your hair is black
and as shiny as the feathers of a raven
I feel its silky coarseness as I run my fingers
    through it.

I take you to the forest
so you can see shade and dappled sunlight
dancing in unison between the northern pines.

We hear the birds chirp and chatter
a chorus of music that never seems to have
    known dismay
nor injustice.

Abandoned to the system
as a young child of four
I promised that I would take care of you well.

Whenever we travel to the sea
we hear the waves crash against the craggy rocks
the wind tousles my hair and likely yours, too.

They tell me the sea is quiet
way down deep
where the struggles to survive
glimpse not the light of day
only darkness
all drama is noiseless
silent.

The drama of our life together
I hope
will be filled with exclamations of joy and few tears.

You are my sweet child now
I shall love you forever
no matter what.

One Night

On the cobblestones
Outside the crumbling Hotel Firenze
I notice a flash of light
And a cigarette breathes life.

I see the slender silhouette of a smoking man
Who does not seem to recognize me
As I slowly saunter by him
With my stilettos sharply striking the stones.

I cough a little to draw attention
And the man looks my way
Then right through me
Though just last night
We were as one.

The Day After I Was Murdered

The day after I was murdered
   I wandered around.
I noticed colours I hadn't seen before
   and heard new sounds.
I followed the footprints of my killer
   away from the spot.
Where I had been strangled
   and left to rot.

The Women on the Subway

I saw a woman
crying
on the subway the other night
dressed all in black
her face was ashen white
with a single tear
rolling down her cheek.

She had a slight, hesitant smile for me
and I wondered what was wrong
what had happened to her
what she was dealing with.

Something passed between us
and for a split second
I seemed not quite so alone
at night
in this strange city
with its smoky haze of neon lights
filtering through the darkness
casting ugly shadows on faces of passersby.

The opportunity was there to reach out
but we let it pass
seemingly unnoticed
but the feeling between us lingered
and again I imagined
that I was not so alone
in this city
on that subway
underground
tunneled in
surrounded by darkness
sounds of screeching rails and demonic souls
echoing through the stillness.

Now, in the train car next to mine
a woman faints
no one around her seems concerned
I stand up to go to her
but the door between cars is locked
she slowly gets up while gently shaking her head
she reaches into her purse
takes out a small box of juice
and begins to sip through a straw.

I watch the colour flow back into her cheeks
she sees me watching her
a slight smile parts her lips
I feel relieved
and not quite so alone
underground
in this strange, dark city
with its smoky haze and grotesque shadows
    encasing me.

To My Son

Just as your hair is dark brown

and your eyes are blue

and your skin is beige

it is part of who you are

and who you are is beautiful.

Aging Ungracefully

Bones need calcium
Brain needs omega 3
Heart needs co-enzyme Q10
Liver needs milk thistle
Face needs sea buckthorn
Vagina needs estrogen
Eyes need lutein
Muscles need human growth factor
Feet need orthotics
Hair needs biotin
Cells need antioxidants
Breasts need lifting and filling
Nose needs sculpting
Cheeks need higher bones
Eyebrows need shaping
Eyelashes need dyeing
Buttocks need implants
Pubic area needs waxing
Abs need tightening
Thighs need toning
Calves need firming

Lips need collagen
Hair needs highlighting
Nails need polishing
Forehead needs smoothing
Under-eye darkness needs erasing.

Industrialized, unattainable 'natural' beauty
Airbrushed for office, home and the streets
Moistness of youth re-injected and resurrected.

A face and body ravaged by weather, experience,
        emotion and exertion
And the steady march of time
Absolutely not acceptable.

Lie of the Lens

Pubescent adolescent?
Not at all.
An adult body houses a frustrated soul.
The look of happiness brings a foregone
    conclusion.
Sweet health, springtime freshness, a glow ebbs
    from the glossy page.

An abduction of the audience.

Upon perceiving this simple photo one assumes
    the subject is carefree.
A self-confidence emanates to uplift sunken
    spirits.

The smile is the key, the eyes begin to sparkle.
The poignancy of the dimples suggest
    suppressed glees of delight.

The effect is suspended there in stillness.

One-sixtieth brings a life-time impression.
Loneliness and insecurity lie beneath this finite
    image.

To capture a moment, a repression of the inner
    soul?

Naked

I was naked
   only a loosely draped sheet covering me
      when you wrapped your hands around my neck
        and told me that you once
           had killed a man with your bare hands.

A Murder of Crows

Throughout the cemetery
The light was beginning to fade
The trees were reflected in shadow
Manicured grass had become straw
Scorched from the blazing summer sun.

A murder of a dozen crows, or so
Gathered as I strolled by
Two shiny, ebony, well-fed ones in front
Began cawing at me
I looked straight at them
They met my eyes with an icy glare in theirs
And attacked.

They flew at me in a single, dark cloud
Then each struck separately
At my face, head, shoulders, neck and chest
Squawking, lunging, pecking, stabbing
I fell to my knees with my head next to the
        ground
Covering the back of my neck with my hands
As taught in class during earthquake drills.

Theodore

The old man walked up the staircase
slowly, deliberately
one foot at a time
taking on each step sideways
only once both feet were firmly on a tread
did he dare lift the other foot
towards the next step
he had fourteen stairs to climb
each night
to his small attic bedroom
it took a good twenty minutes to summit his
    Everest
with three or four rest stops
of a few minutes each.

While ascending
the old man looked down
at both of his hands
as they gripped the bannister
tightly, securely, intently
he gazed at his hands
with new disbelief each night
as he saw

that his once sensuous, strong, masculine hands
the ones his wife would kiss each morning to
    greet him and the day
had become so thin
like ten long, knobbly, crooked sticks
sporting chipped and cracked nail ends
bony spurs on knuckles where cartilage used to
    be hidden and intact
years of hard labour on his property had
    gifted him
these disfigured, grotesque, arthritic fingers
it wasn't when he was climbing the stairs
it wasn't when he looked in his mirror
it wasn't when his knees and back creaked each
    morning as he rose out of bed
that he was reminded he was old
it was glancing at his hands which brought a
    sudden flash of the years
which had gone before
and the few that were left ahead.

Margaret had been dead now for just over seven
    years
his soul ached for her still
all he was doing without her was surviving
he wasn't really living
he certainly wasn't thriving
just going through each daily motion as if
    suspended in liquid
or in a mist
or a fog
nothing seemed clear to him anymore.

He and Margaret had no children
no grandchildren
he had employed a cleaning woman for a couple
    of years
but she left when she turned sixty-three
because her back and knees couldn't take the
    physicality of the work anymore
or the stairs for that matter.

A couple of nights back
the old man had tripped on the top stair
nearly plummeting downwards, sideways
he had gripped the bannister hard while gritting
    his teeth
and was able to stop the tumble from happening
he hadn't banged his head on anything
but had seen yellow and white stars anyhow
he had felt Margaret's spirit nearby
and was able to unburden himself to her
about how frightened he had been
while at the same time longing to be with her.

Tonight he went straight to his bed without
    washing up
laying first on his back
then rolling onto his side
cradling himself by pulling his knees to his chest
and wrapping his arms around them
he felt agonizingly lonely
and filled with despair

he quelled his urge to scream
as the heartbreak of loss became too much for
     him to bear
at 3 a.m. when he still couldn't sleep
he rose and put an old Johnny Cash record on the
     turntable
he still enjoyed *Folsom Prison Blues*
he used to cradle Margaret in his arms
while they both sat in the tattered, over-sized
armchair in the living room
listening to Johnny Cash's deep growl.

Margaret had also liked some of the more
     modern music
that the twenty-something kids listened to
and used to dance around the kitchen while
     preparing dinner
with the latest hits blaring on FM radio as her
     inspiration
she seemed so very young at heart
most of the time
no matter what was happening at any moment of
     any day
and that is what he absolutely adored about her
along with the mischievous twinkle in her bright
     blue
her azure
eyes
deep pools of love the colour of the
     Mediterranean sea
as he imagined it to be
if it mirrored his idea of a perfect sky.

Margaret would never dance in public
no matter how much he tried to coax her into
     doing so
she was terribly self-conscious in front of
     everyone
and only ever allowed him
and only him
to see her at her best
her most lively
her most captivating and daring
not even at their wedding had she taken a spin or
     a twirl
they had skipped the traditional bride and groom
     dance
settling instead on watching their guests
some of whom were heavily liquored-up
prance and parade around the dance floor.

What made Margaret self-conscious about
     dancing
even though she could be quite graceful and lithe
     on her feet
were her mismatched legs
one of her legs was almost half an inch shorter
     than the other
she had a shoe with a lift in it
but never felt secure enough in it to chance
     dancing in front of others
she had to admit that she even felt self-conscious
     at times
while at home with her husband
sometimes feeling shame more than just
     self-consciousness.

Still there were plenty of marvellous times at
    home over the years
when they danced and twirled long enough for
    her to feel wild abandon
laughing and singing along to the music
so that she soon forgot all about her legs
and during those times she radiated exquisite
    perfection
transcendent beauty
the music and her husband's love carried her
    away to another time
to another place
to a more glamorous life
perhaps to the ballroom of a grand old mansion.

Pain

I took the blade
   slashed my arm
doused my hair in oil
   mixed in some warm blood
smearing it all over my scalp
   and the rest of my nakedness.

I scrubbed ruthlessly with my fingernails
   slicing my scalp
and the rest of my body
   whimpering like a wounded animal
while trying to push away the queasiness
   in the pit of my stomach.

Purging
   rinsing
eradicating stench and memory.

The Prairie Bread Basket

The sun is beginning its descent towards the
    horizon
as I cycle along beside a field of wheat.

Some of the flaxen-tipped cereal grass has been
    carefully compressed
and tightly rolled for transport.

I stop for a while.

I inhale the sweet, clean, prairie air deep into my
    lungs
as I celebrate ancestors who emigrated from
    Europe's bread basket
to this bread basket of Canada decades ago.

Eejit Perhaps

Each day, upon rising
I ask myself if I am, in fact, an idiot
An eejit
A moron
A stupide person
An idiota.
My answer differs from day to day.

You and Me

Do you know who I am
Do you really listen to a word that I say
Or do you see me how you think I should be
As a woman
As a daughter
As a mother
As a wife
Are you willing to listen
To hear?

I'd like to explain to you
How and who I really am
And that I am happy being me
Or at least trying to be me.

Part Two

Haikus

Fat Crow Pecked

Fat crow pecked at eaves
black mulch of leaves splashed downward
just missed your bald spot.

Grey Gorillas

Tropical forests
house silver-grey gorillas
romping mightily.

Act of Terror

Shrapnel, bodies, blood
sirens scream loud on approach
horrific terror.

Wheat

Driving by green-tipped
flaxen wheat rippled by breeze
sharp hail shreds tassels.

Winter Wonderland

Peering through the trees
at our winter wonderland
time to ski powder.

Old Woman

Old woman was cold
she huddled in smoky haze
no homestead for years.

Harbinger of Spring

Harbinger of spring
arrived early amid snow
a red-breasted chap.

The Pond

Pond's glinting surface
lightly cat-paw across it
until ice crackles.

Black-capped Chickadee

Black-capped chickadee
nips at the blood-red berries
juicy sustenance.

Threatening Storm

Low dark clouds threaten
wind whistles through the poplars
pulse subtly quickens.

Dark-eyed Junco

The dark-eyed junco
visits as the snow recedes
white tail feathers twitch.

Weapons of War

Perusing headlines
monstrous violence against girls
rape as a weapon.

Hummingbird

Above pink fuchsia
hummingbirds fight each other
for sweet succulence.

WestJet Flight

WestJet flight skids off
YYZ taxiway strip
stuck in snow for hours.

Dastardly Rodent

Bulbs yanked from the soil
tender shoots nibbled and frayed
dastardly rodent.

Valentine's Day

This Valentine's day
remember the origins
dark, red and bloody.

Eagle Grabs Salmon

An eagle swoops down
grabs a salmon from my boat
incredible gall.

Broken Tooth

Chomps down on almond
middle tooth cracks and splinters
gosh darn dental bills.

Arctic Front

A brisk Arctic front
pushes forcefully inland
frigid, bitter cold.

San Francisco Tram

Riding the tram up
steep hills of San Francisco
we slice through cool mist.

Kindness

Anger and hatred
destroy human peace of mind
err towards kindness.

Strong Winds

Strong winds are anon
snow wafts gently like feathers
until the storm hits.

About the Author

Deborah K. Hanula has a year of Journalism training, a Political Science degree from the University of Waterloo, and a Law degree from the University of British Columbia. In addition, she has diplomas in Cognitive Behavioural Therapy, Child Psychology, and Psychotherapy and Counselling, as well as certificates in Family Life Education and Coaching, Reflexology, Assertiveness Training and Mindfulness Meditation. She was an early creator of recipes that contain no gluten or dairy and went on to compile those recipes in a few cookbooks. She has worked primarily as a lawyer, but also as a university and college lecturer, tutor, editor, writer, counsellor, researcher and piano teacher. She enjoys a multi-faceted approach when it comes to life, work and study in order to keep things fresh and interesting. She has written several blogs which can be found at <u>blogger.com</u> under a "psyche and mind" heading. Additional blogs display some of her photography.

9 780228 888208